RELIGION TEACHER'S PET

by

Marie McIntyre

100 self-help ideas for creative catechists

Layout, design and artwork by Maryann Read

Library of Congress Catalog Card 78-65637
ISBN 0-89622-088-5

CONTENTS

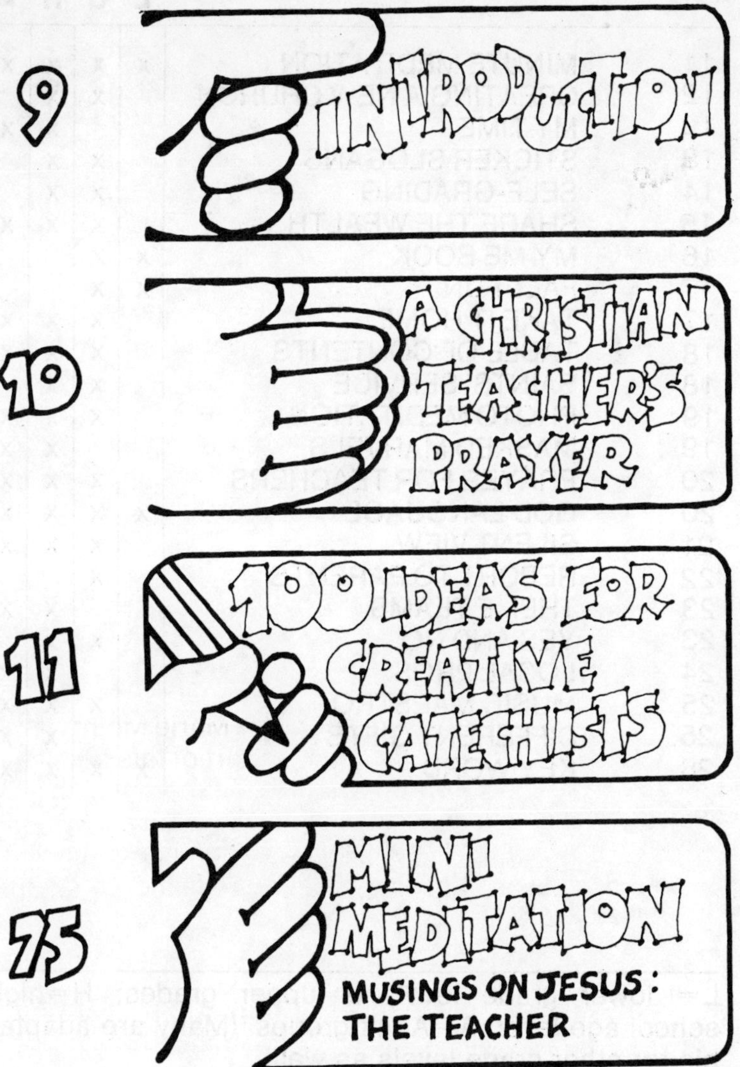

INTRODUCTION
A CHRISTIAN TEACHER'S PRAYER
100 IDEAS FOR CREATIVE CATECHISTS
MINI MEDITATION
MUSINGS ON JESUS:
THE TEACHER

CONTENTS

L= lower grade level; U=upper grades; H=high school age level; A=Adult groups. (Many are adaptable for other grade levels as well)

L= lower grade level; U=upper grades; H=high school age level; A=Adult groups. (Many are adaptable for other grade levels as well)

INTRODUCTION

What can this little book do for a catechist or religion teacher? Well, we presume that you want very much to create happy and comfortable, yet serious and challenging opportunities to help those you teach "grow in wisdom and grace before God and all people." We also know that the hectic pace of life today keeps most teachers from having the leisure time you would love to have for more thoughtful and better class preparation. So, we've put together a collection of 100 creative and helpful ideas that you can easily adapt to your local situation. In the table of contents, we've indicated the age level most appropriate for them but adaptations very easily can be made to modify them for use at lower or upper grade levels.

These examples of activity suggestions are offered in the hope of spurring you to create your own learning situations and stimulate your own creative juices so that you will truly enjoy both the privilege and the responsibility of sharing the good news that Jesus is God's prime sacrament of His love for us.

After each suggestion, you will find a space to record date and class or group with whom you used the idea or technique. This record will be a help if you happen to have the same people in your class or group the following year.

We have also offered a prayer before teaching and a few reflections on Jesus as teacher for your quiet times when you are preparing or reflecting on your task as a parish catechist or a classroom religion teacher. We hope this little book proves to be helpful and hope-filled enough to encourage you to "hang in there" because your faith and your example of "caring enough to give the very best" is your gift to those you teach. God loves you for this.

A Christian Teacher's Prayer

It's prayer time, Lord.
It's time for us to speak
each to the other, yet
You know so well to listen
beyond my groping words. . . .

My mind's a grasshopper, Lord.
It hops and skips around.
It's filled with thoughts of duties
which infringe upon this
precious contact time with You.
Yet, I speak to ask You, Lord
to teach me how to teach!

Let your Spirit guide me
to distill the best of all
the struggling words that strive
to speak in awe of You.

Let Your Spirit fashion phrases
that will move the hearts
of those I teach so that
my time with them will be
great seconds of salvation—
freeing them and freeing me.

And, listen, Lord, to this:
As I try to "speak the truth in love"
may Your love leap out of me
to warm and unify my class
and help each person present
know that learning more of You
prepares the way for life
lived in the loving service
which brings the peace and joy
You promised us the night before
You gave your all for us.

1
Minute Meditation

The habit of quiet meditation before beginning a class is a good one. If you have a record player or cassette recorder, select some soft, soothing music to play quietly as the group assembles and settles down. Suggest a meditation topic in one or two words such as: *Jesus, time, gratefulness, Mary, baptism, thoughtfulness, selfishness,* etc. Eventually, meditation time can be an opportunity for sharing and a time of praise.

It is very important that you meditate with the group and not "be busy about many things" at your desk instead. Our actions are real conveyers of our values. Quietly turn off the music at the end of the prayer period.

Date: _________________ Class/group: _______________

2
Creating A New Church

Early in the school year, ask the children to tell you all they think about when you say "church." Put these words or phrases on the board and then lead a discussion about these. Then, erase everything and ask the children to pretend that up to this moment, there is no church but that it is their task to create one.

Let them think about this and then put their ideas or phrases on the board. Note what remains important and to be "kept" from their past experience and note anything creative and what this could mean for the future church.

This experience will help you know where the children "are coming from" and who are the potential leaders in the group. It will also highlight misconceptions and remedial work you will have to incorporate into your lessons in order to build a better foundation for the future.

Date: _______________ Class/group: _______________

3
My Time

In this age when people complain that they don't have enough time to do what they want, try this: Ask each person to mark off a page into 30 squares to represent a typical calendar month. Now tell them that each has the power to design this calendar the way s/he would really like time to be. One may want nine Sundays in the month; another may wish to have all Saturdays, etc. Each, however, must write into the squares what they plan to do with this free gift of time. After a sufficient time, conduct a discussion on what each wanted most time for. Analyse how much of this time was planned to be with or of service to other people, whether or not "time spent making money" had a real priority, how much time went for celebration, worship, being alone, hobbies, sports, study, etc. Ask each person to draw private conclusions about time and how we waste it, use it, etc. A follow-up from this exercise should be more appreciation for the importance of personal decisions and responsibility for accepting the gift of time.

Date: _________________ Class/group: _________________

4
Sticker Slogans

In this culture where bumper stickers and slogans are so popular, encourage students to search the scriptures or their literature lessons for significant quotations. Suggest that they condense these into as few words as possible and design one or more of these into car bumper stickers or window or bulletin board slogans. Have a slogan parade around the room to celebrate the completion of the activity.

Date: _________________ Class/group: _________________

5
Self-Grading

To help establish responsibility on the part of each student, suggest that each grade his or her own work on the basis of the following questions:

1) Did I really do my best on this assignment?
(A B C D E)

2) Did I do anything over and above the assignment to help me achieve more than was asked by the teacher?
(A B C D E)

3) Am I doing this work because I want to deepen my understanding of my religion and prepare to be a better Christian?
(A B C D E)

Date: _________________ Class/group: _________________

6
Share the Wealth

Place a $1.00 bill on the floor in the center of a circle of people. Tell them that it is really a $1,000.00 bill. Each person present is responsible for doing something with it. Give them time to write down how they would invest, share, use, give away, or spend the money. Hold a discussion on the results and analyse the real relationship to money revealed by this group. It would be very helpful to repeat the assignment now with this statement, "This $1,000.00 is now YOURS. Do you still have the same thoughts about its use, disposal, investment, etc.? How does "mine" and "thine" make a difference? Should it? Why? Etc. Many values can spin off from a project like this.

Date: ________________ Class/group: ________________

7
My ME Book

Good teaching demands that we know our children and their individual needs and differences. To become more sensitively aware of each child, encourage each to make a ME book. Supply materials and crayolas or felt tip pens and tell them that they will add to their book, bit by bit, each week. They are to choose their favorite colors and do a MY BOOK cover design. Tell them to include pages about their families, home, pets, birthdays, favorite celebrations, hobbies, etc. The emerging picture will help children to know themselves and the gifts God has given them and will make a great keepsake to take home eventually.

These books introduce the teacher to the uniqueness of each child and will help you to appreciate his or her strengths, weaknesses, cultural background, faith environment, etc. This is a helpful "getting to know you" aid to keep teachers aware that each class is like a garden with a genuine variety of flowers all of which cannot be treated exactly alike.

Date: _______________ Class/group: _______________

8
Fall Fun

In order to encourage children to appreciate God's creation, have them read, meditate, and discuss Psalm 104. Then, unroll several feet of shelf or wrapping paper allocating a portion to each child. Each is to fill his or her space with magazine photos, illustrations, or original art indicating some creation for which he or she is grateful. The resulting panorama can then be used as a visual aid when the class later returns to Psalm 104.

Date: _________________ Class/group: _________________

9
Take It Home

People usually learn best when they have to organize new material or information in such a way as to pass it on to others. Assign as a homework project that the members of the class do a lesson plan on how to relay your present topic or theme to 1) younger children at home; 2) peers; 3) parents or adult friends.

Date: _________________ Class/group: _________________

10
Table of Contents

A very challenging task which can be adapted for most age levels except the very young is to ask each person to prepare a table of contents for the "catechism" s/he would like to present to his/her children as the core of basic beliefs, values, and practices that really have meaning for a contemporary Christian. Do the first rough draft in class or in a group but then ask each person to take the outlines home, think them over, revise them, and try to present a finished and satisfactory outline at the following meeting. These outlines can become the basis for lesson outlines for the year and are valuable for keeping and comparing when the same challenge is given a year or two later.

Date: _______________ Class/group: ______ ________

11
Saints' Service

To prepare for All Saints Day, have each student research his or her favorite saint. Prepare a one-page report to be shared with the class highlighting some specific service that the saint performed for the church of his or her time. The rest of the students who hear the report are to offer practical ways to translate that particular service into actions that the class can perform here and now in their own time and environment.

Date: _______________ Class/group: _______________

12
Photo Meditation

Display two or three large contemporary scene photos relating to the theme of your class. Ask the students to write the "cut lines" or poem-prayer-phrases resulting from meditation on the photo of their choice. At the end of class, have them turn over the sheet on which they wrote the original meditation lines and tell them to now write a new set which should reflect the content of the lesson and any new insights as a result. Ask for volunteers to read some of these as the closing prayer for class.

Date: _______________ Class/group: _______________

13
Masked Marvels

October is an easy time to focus on masks. Prior to Halloween, however, a discussion on why people wear masks and what happens to people when they wear masks can be helpful. Encourage students to admit that we have psychological masks, also, when we "put on a different face" from our true internal attitude. The "why" may lead to such answers as "fear," "shame," "embarrassment." Discuss how we can help one another not to wear masks but to be comfortable with being our real selves.

Date: _________________ Class/group: _________________

14
Prayer for Teachers

After a meeting on understanding and sharing, invite all to enter a "BEST PRAYER FOR TEACHER" contest. Announce that the best ones will be used occasionally in class but be sure to note the recurring themes and expectations that occur in these prayers. Trying to live up to these ideals and hopes will be your challenge and your guide.

Date: _________________ Class/group: _________________

15
God Language

For younger children, use the blackboard, Older children can write the words themselves in their own books. Begin by asking children to tell or write the adjectives or words they think about when you say "candy." For example, sweet, sugar, tasty, yum-yum, chewy, etc. may come forth. Repeat this for "water" or something else which is common. Now repeat it for "God." You may get words like: creator, trinity, love, judge, father, supreme being, spirit, etc. Ask the class to select the word from the list that would best describe God for them and discuss why some words have far more truth-meaning in them than others. This technique is a good one when beginning any material which may be fairly new to the group in order to find out what the presuppositions are and where the vacuums are. It is also good to point out that while none of our words are adequate, many of them are good pointers to the truth and no words really are totally adequate when it comes to describing faith realities.

Date: _______________ Class/group: _______________

16
Silent View

Show a filmstrip without the accompanying sound. Ask each person to jot down the possible theme, dialogue, key action, etc. Then, show the filmstrip with the soundtrack. Compare the original imagined message with the audio or the second showing. Discuss such values as: how we learn, how we judge with incomplete information, how imagination sometimes teaches us more than factual information, etc. This becomes an invaluable learning device if you are using a filmstrip about a key belief or practice.

Date: _______________ Class/group: _________________

NEWS FLASH

17

Report to Parents

During the last 10 minutes of class some day, ask the students to become instant reporters with only a minute or two to file their stories on what went on in class that day. Have one student write the "headlines" on the blackboard and then have all in the group copy them and take them home to share with their parents. For example, "Class learns names of 12 Apostles" or "Mary Brown, student teacher, showed map of Palestine during Jesus' lifetime" or "Mrs. Jones told story about Good Samaritan." This brief report technique serves to review and summarize the class material and also to bridge the communication gap between school and home.

Date: _______________ Class/group: _________________

18
Theme Teams

To encourage working together, learning together, and the experience of discovering that sharing and cooperation is much more humanizing than individual competition, break the class into several teams. For example, prior to or during a study of the sacraments, break into seven teams, each of which is assigned a particular sacrament to research for historical background, liturgical trends, contemporary theology, etc. Illustrate with posters, banners, montages, music, etc. Each week, a different team presents a report in the form of a radio or TV program. Be sure to leave plenty of time for recreation-discussion by the rest of the class and to clarify anything that may require modification or special help. Commandments, prayer phrases, basic beliefs, etc. can go to theme teams.

Date: _________________ Class/group: _______________

19
Yes and No

Play a values game with the children. Have half of the group write statements on index cards on how to celebrate Advent, Christmas, etc. The other half is to respond with a YES or a NO to each statement and then to give the reason for their choice.

Date: _________________ Class/group: _______________

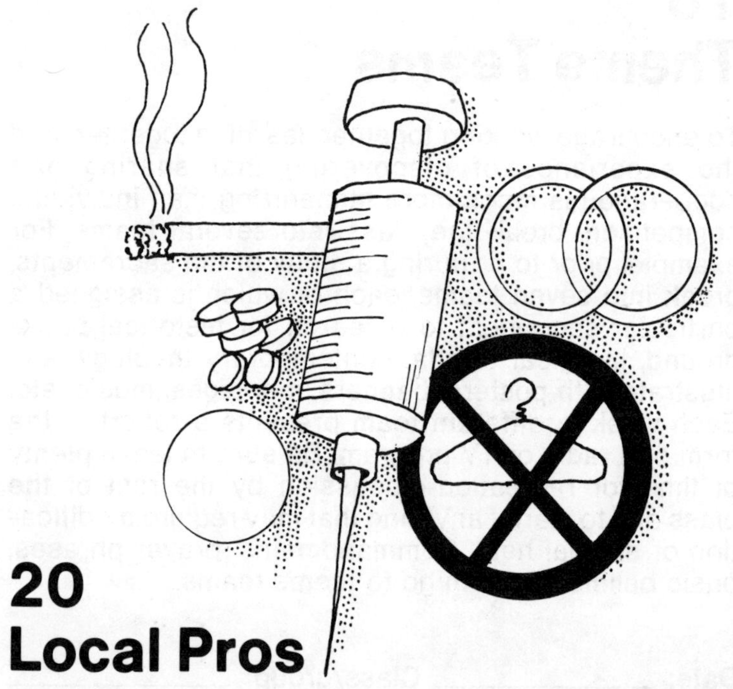

20
Local Pros

Plan a program of learning from the "professionals" in your midst. Students can be assigned to discover local talent and invite people to a sharing session. For example, friends, relatives and neighbors could well include a doctor who would be willing to explain the doctor's dilemma in life/death situations, a lawyer who could offer practical advice regarding willing money for charitable use, a marriage counsellor who could describe early symptoms of alienation which need immediate attention, an administrator who runs a home for the elderly, etc. Make up a list of topics most people want to know more about such as money, friendships, loneliness, drugs, etc. and take it from there.

Date: _______________ Class/group: _______________

21
Music Maestro

Each is to write a "hit song" for the following week's theme, be it Thanksgiving, Advent, Christmas, Easter, etc. Encourage the students to write their own words to a well-known tune. The class may vote on which song best portrays the season, the event, the theme.

Date: _______________ Class/group: _______________

22
Different Gifts

To show how God's word can be enriched for us when all the people of God share in being open to receive it, select a theme from the bible for a homily or a sermon. Cluster into groups of three or four all-male, all-female groups. Each group is to compose a "sermon" on the theme. Have one spokesman or spokeswoman for each group read the results. Then, discuss the significant patterns that emerge when men ponder on God's word and when women do so. Have the group discuss the value of having both men and women participate and what value this could have for the future church.

Date: _________________ Class/group: _________________

23
Key Word

Here's a meditation and value technique that can be adapted for any season of the year. For example, if it is Christmas, write several words on the board that relate to the common experience of all: bells, tree, gifts, shopping, carols, etc. or for Easter: bunny, clothes, church, candle, etc. Let each student select the word which is most meaningful to him or her and write it on a piece of paper along with a sentence or two explaining why this word was chosen. Encourage them to choose a word of their own if they are not satisfied with the quality of the list on the board. The aim of this exercise is to stimulate thinking and discussion about the deeper meaning of the feast, the event, or the topic.

Date: _________________ Class/group: _________________

24
Homily Telegrams

A good Monday or early-in-the-week assignment is to ask each student to "send a telegram" to a friend reporting in as few words as possible the real value and meaning of Sunday's homily. Besides encouraging a careful listening attitude, the task will foster the discipline of selecting the right words to get to the core truth. Vary the telegram idea with the suggestion that the key message be put into a four-line poem instead.

Date: _________________ Class/group: _________________

25
Knowing

What does it mean to *know?* How do we *really know?* What are some of the ways the word "know" is used in the bible? After a discussion and discovery about knowing, point out how important it is that we know one another. Ask the class to pose three questions they would like to ask about another person in class. Write the questions on the board and then vote as a group for the top three questions. Next, spend a few minutes letting the students get to "know one another" through these questions. This is important to do early in the school year, particularly in groups where many new people appear who were not in the neighborhood the year before. After this activity, assign as a meditation and motivation that they look up John 17:3 and relate their new awareness of knowing persons to the implications of this passage.

Date: _________________ Class/group: _________________

26
On Assignment

As a pre-Christmas (or Easter, Pentecost, etc.) project assign the responsibility of preparing a Christmas tabloid insert for the local paper. Students should be encouraged to collect all the items they can find out about Christmas around the world, do their own layout, draw their own pictures to illustrate the articles and compose their own headlines. The finished "magazine" can become a gift to the parents on Christmas morning.

Date: _________________ Class/group: _________________

27
Winter Week

Instead of thinking of vacation time as something entirely for self, have the class list all the things which can be done around the house to help parents enjoy a vacation from their usual tasks. Place some of these on slips of paper in little boxes to be gift-wrapped as presents to hang on the tree. These "promise gifts" can be fulfilled during Christmas vacation week before school resumes. Adapt for Easter or other times during the year and enlarge the idea to include needy, handicapped, and elderly neighbors.

Date: _________________ Class/group: _________________

28
Good News Litany

Ask the children to collect any headlines during the week that relate good news for which all can be grateful. Assign a committee of volunteers to collect these and organize them into a litany of thanksgiving. Then, appoint two or three good readers to take turns reading the headlines and ask the class to respond, "For this good news, we thank You, Lord." Hopefully, the selected headlines will reflect social and political events that promote justice, peace, and the common good.

Date: _________________ Class/group: _________________

29
Person Giving

Before Christmas, have the class compose a list of gifts which are "person-to-person" and not "thing things." For example, the gift of an hour of my time to help you with your work, the gift of my muscles to help you shovel snow, the gift of my sight to read to the blind, the gift of my favorite TV program when yours comes on at the same time, the gift of presence when you are confined to bed or in a nursing home, the gift of my homemade favorite recipe because you can't cook, etc. Suggest that as an alternative to buying things people do not need, the class celebrates the Presence of Jesus among us by being Jesus present to others now.

Date: _________________ Class/group: _________________

30
And Also For You

A man makes a promise to donate to the poor the price of every luxury he enjoys for himself: beer, cigarettes, movies, etc. He does this in the belief that Jesus is present in the needs of those who have less than he has. He says, "Matt. 25:40 is too important to ignore." Have the class discuss this attitude, and Matt. 25:40 and a group consensus action-reaction. Discuss what the world would be like if the man who makes the promise turns out to be every man and woman in town ... and even if this happened for only one year of each person's life.

Date: _______________ Class/group: _______________

31
Favorite Song Lines

Have each member of the class select two to four lines from a favorite current hit record and bring to class a report on the meaning and message communicated. Have them indicate whether they agree with the value or message portrayed and whether they have made or wish to make this value part of their own lives. This assignment should encourage a critical listening to the words of the songs and an understanding of how these words can affect peoples' thinking and acting.

Date: _______________ Class/group: _______________

32
Draw and Pray

Give each student a blank sheet of plain typing paper and ask them to design a placemat for the table. In the center, they are to print or write a prayer of their own for before or after meals. Post these around the room so that others can share and be helped by the prayers. Let the students vote for the best three by a silent ballot. Encourage students to take their own placemats home for use at mealtimes. Remind them that they could make up sets with different prayers on better quality paper to be used as gifts for family or friends at different times of the year.

Date: _______________ Class/group: _______________

33
Resolution Revolution

The traditional time for making resolutions is New Year's Day. This year, plan a "revolution day" instead of a "resolution day." Have the students meet in groups of four to six to plan a "revolution for good"—an activity in which all can be involved and which will improve the condition of others. This will help them understand that community is formed when people are unified in purpose and activity and that we all need others to promote the common good.

Date: _______________ Class/group: _______________

34
The Year that Was

In January, plan a "year that was" review class. Assign groups of pupils the task of producing a skit or visual to review the key lessons learned since September. Tie these together by simulating a TV show and have a Master of Ceremonies or teacher to introduce each "act"—highlights of the key themes since September.

Date: ________________ Class/group: ________________

35
Earth Matters

To help foster ongoing care for the diminishing natural resources, hold a "fuel saver" contest. Winner is the person who can prove that his/her idea does work and does save fuel or other dwindling resources in school, home, or public places. Remind them that saving fuel "costs" is not the goal. It is not the money one saves but the resource itself with a resulting attitude toward conserving for the sake of others.

Date: ________________ Class/group: ________________

36
Happy Hour

Fun time can be creative and community-forming. Make duplicate copies of several cartoons without cut-lines and pass these around the room. Each person is to write the quip line that goes under the cartoon. After the sharing session, lead the group to realize the value of having fun together and the resulting change of attitudes for some. For older groups, discuss the value of play and celebration and the relationship contemplation has to play. At any rate, take time out for fun.

Date: _________________ Class/group: _________________

37
Question Box

After a class presentation, ask each who wishes to do so, to put a question in the box relating to the theme or subject under discussion. Then ask volunteer "instant teachers" to withdraw a question and attempt to answer it. Classmates are then invited (most of them won't wait for the invitation) to agree or disagree with the answer, to clarify it, to add to it, and so on. This review technique creates a challenge and a great deal of participation.

Date: _______________ Class/group: _______________

38
All Gifts All the Time

An outstanding characteristic of Jesus is his relationship of loving gratitude to his Father. To help students appreciate that even the things we take for granted are gifts, encourage "reflect-response" times. For example, ask them to write a few poem phrases about something as common as a piece of bread. Share these reflections in class and discover even more reasons for being grateful.

Date: _________________ Class/group: _________________

39
Class Twinning

If you are in a school or CCD program where there is another class of your age or grade group, work with the other teacher to plan a co-op program. To encourage more cooperation and less competition, have each group do part of a project such as a New Testament mural, a program for parents, a visitation plan for the housebound, senior citizens, etc. Cooperation in preparing liturgies for specific occasions will help prepare students for parish council commissions in the future.

Date: _________________ Class/group: _________________

40
Valentine Hour

Children, like adults, need encouragement in expressing affection for those they love, especially family members. Try having a VALENTINE HOUR during which time each is to design little note cards with "Name_____, I love you because...." in the heart drawn or printed on the outside of the card. Inside, ask them to write a reason or two for each member of the family. Fill in the name in the blank on the outside of the card and place cards at each family member's place at breakfast on Feb. 14.

Date: _________________ Class/group: _________________

41
Take-A-Turn Teaching

In order to stimulate creative sharing, assign to two or three students at a time, the task of being "teacher" for a portion of the next class. Encourage them to use any technique, audio-visual, or helpful learning idea they may wish. As you become the "learner" in this situation, note what each student considers the highlight of the particular lesson or assignment. While students are having the opportunity to face a group in public, you can learn a great deal by listening and observing. When you do this with high school and adult groups, you quickly discover potential teachers for the future, too.

Date: _________________ Class/group: _________________

42
Prophets

Select three or four Old Testament prophets and assign to each member of the group the task of learning more about these prophets, their history, their cultural environment, their message. Then, find a person in today's world who most resembles one of these prophets in a similar situation and with a similar message. After this, discuss why prophets are necessary and good for society at all times and in all places.

Date: _______________ Class/group: _______________

43
Prepare for Lent

Assign teams of students to approach Parish Council liturgy committee members with suggestions for your parish's Lenten program. Do this in January or earlier in order to stimulate committees who are not yet making plans or to give support to those who are. Most committee members need to hear what the younger members of the parish feel they need for better worship experiences.

Date: _________________ Class/group: _________________

44
Lent for Loving

The negative concept of "giving up" for Lent can be transformed into "giving to" if we encourage children to "think neighbor" during Lent. Hold a class discussion on how each member of the class can do a "give to" activity for Lent. Assign a secretary to list these suggestions on a bulletin board. Ask students to make a check mark after the activity listed each time this is accomplished. The witness value of the group participation in the project is important and faith-supporting.

Date: _________________ Class/group: _________________

45
Centering In Silence

Encourage total quiet and relaxation for a class prayer period. Show the students how to relax by putting feet flat on floor, palms of hands down on tops of desks, back erect, and eyes gazing at one spot straight ahead. Soft background music should be played while the students are encouraged to relax and to be completely alone with God for a few minutes. This centering in silence is a good way to encourage the members of the class to take time out each day at home or elsewhere to talk to God.

Date: _________________ Class/group: _________________

46
Lent Log

Forty days can be a long time for children—or for anyone. Suggest a "progress report" in the form of a personal LENT LOG. Each student may keep a personal report of how his/her preparation for Easter is progressing. Be certain to suggest positive rather than negative activities. Have the children suggest to the class what they feel the Lent Log should contain.

Date: _________________ Class/group: _________________

47
Other Christians

As the ecumenical spirit grows on the grassroots level, it is important to help eliminate prejudices and foster understanding. Work with Christian teachers from other churches toward a sharing session or a visit to a class being held at the same time in another church. Then, invite return visits and discussions. In locales where professionals are available, sponsor a panel discussion at these times with questions from the group. These meetings always reveal how much we have in common with other churches and how difficult it is for most people to comprehend the real significance of the theological differences.

Date: _________________ Class/group: _______________

48
Other Religions

As the world becomes a global village at a faster pace than ever before, take advantage of any opportunity to prepare your students for the world they will live in with its countless belief systems. Invite representatives of non-Christian religions to speak to your group and be available for a question period, or take class trips to synagogues, temples, and other worship places when possible and feasible. Before doing so, though, reading something like Dorothy Dixon's *World Religions for the Classroom* would be very helpful.

Date: _______________ Class/group: _______________

49
Process Story

A technique that keeps children absorbed and learning begins with a flannelboard. Make your own with a yard of flannelette stretched tightly over a piece of cardboard. Prop it on a slight slant such as on the chalk container and against the blackboard. Pass around felt cut-outs of the characters in the story you are telling. When you finish, invite someone to retell the story and have each child with a cut-out "prop" come up and place it on the flannelboard at the appropriate time. This serves to keep all interested as the visual unfolds before the eyes of those who do not have a specific, active part in the retelling. Obviously, flannelboards have a variety of uses. This is just one. You can think of many more.

Date: _______________ Class/group: _______________

50
Rap Trap

Obtain end rolls of newsprint from your local newspaper and tape the roll along a wall. Use a wide felt-tip pen and write out a "rap trap" unfinished sentence such as: "In our church, I'm really bothered by....." "If I could change one thing, I would....." Ask people to walk up and write their completion to the sentence selected. Emotions and attitudes are thus expressed and can become the basis for a rap session which can lead to positive action.

Date: _______________ Class/group: _______________

51
Weekly Paper

If you are in a situation where you have the same group each day, plan for a Friday edition of a class paper (or once-a-month paper if you have weekly classes). Assign editors, reporters, artists, etc. to "cover" each class so that the staff will be able to put together a "class paper" which will highlight the key themes of the week and the significant experiences of the class. Include best homework hero, best "pupil teacher," etc.

Encourage those who are not on the "staff" this time to contribute poems, posters, cartoons, drawings, etc. to the staff. Next time, rotate the class paper staff so that others will have the opportunity of working together on the project. Any "working together project" will help students experience group and community effort and the discipline involved to make such activity fruitful.

Date: _________________ Class/group: _______________

52
Super Slueth

Assign each person a scripture passage related to the theme of the class or meeting. Each is to look for as many clues as possible in local newspapers and magazines which relate to this passage. The "super slueth" must then turn in a report about what this investigation revealed about how the biblical theme relates to life as we live it today.

Date: _________________ Class/group: _______________

53
Teacher Feature

Assign to each student two minutes to be teacher at the next session. This encourages creativity on the part of the individual and also the discipline of condensing what is important into small segments of time thus eliminating the fluff and getting to the heart of the matter. Have the rest of the class verbalize whether the student teacher was effective or not and why. The "why" is the important thing. These reasons will indicate what your students are looking for in you, too.

Date: _________________ Class/group: _________________

54
I Really Hate . . . .

As the dark side of our lives is often repressed, hidden, ignored, etc., it is important for basic health and truth to face our total selves and explore the deep caves within us. Ask the children to write down a list of "hates," discontents, aversions, etc. Then, group these into "can do something about" and "can't do anything about" columns. Personal meditation on these columns will cause a shifting about and an awareness that we can do a great deal to modify our attitudes, prejudices, selfishness, pride, etc. and the underlying causes of these "hates." This is a basic exercise leading to a real examination of conscience and the awareness of the need for daily, continuous conversion.

Date: _________________ Class/group: _________________

55
Talent Gift Box

To help people understand that each person has a gift to share for the good of all, place a pretty gift box in the room and then ask each person to write down on a slip of paper a talent s/he has that can be shared. A good voice, ability to organize, thoughtful listening to someone's problems, etc. are some suggestions to get them started. Then, ask each person to write the name of a talent of someone else in the room. Put all of these "gifts" into the gift box and then have someone draw them out and read them. Follow this by a reading and meditation on the parable of the talents in Matt. 25.

Date: _______________ Class/group: _______________

56
Letters From God

Everyone has a bible. Everyone has a piece of notepaper. Allow about 10 minutes in which each is to search for a message or a passage in the bible that will contain a "love message" when sent to someone. Copy that passage and sign the letter from God. Fold up and exchange with others in the room. As each opens his/her love note from God, the power of the Good News will be experienced in a new way. Here are a few examples: John 8:32. John 14:1. Matt. 5:9. Mark 9:35. Luke 3:11.

Date: _______________ Class/group: _______________

57
Telephone Report

Toward the end of class, remind the group that someone is absent and missed the experience of learning
and celebrating that day. Ask someone to volunteer to
phone the missing person and explain what happened
and what was learned, experienced, discovered.
Attach a string to a nob for an imaginary phone line and
ask the rest of the class to "listen in" as the volunteer
"phones" his/her absent friend. After the volunteer
hangs up, let anyone else add what may have been
missed or should have been highlighted.

Date: _________________ Class/group: _______________

58
Preparing the Way

Here's a technique to get a more intense participation from students on any grade level. Assign as a homework task a "preview of coming attractions." Tell the class that the theme or topic for the following month will be _________ and then ask all to do advance research on that topic so that on the first day for this theme, each will be invited to share what he or she has already discovered about the topic. For example, if your subject is what recent popes have said about war, announce this and let each student report on what sources were used in the research and what was discovered.

Date: _______________ Class/group: _______________

59
My Name as Pope

When Pope John Paul I took the names of both his predecessors, he was telling the world that he had admiration for both men and their efforts as the chief servant of the church. Let each person present imagine that s/he is a newly elected pope. What name would s/he take? Why? This will lead to discussion, research, and a new awareness of the tremendous responsibility the pope has.

Date: _______________ Class/group: _______________

60
Spring Song

As new life begins to show itself in nature, encourage a conscious response to the miracle of life by having a "spring song contest." Children may compose their own music or write their own words to popular melodies. When all are ready, the performance can be given with the class casting a secret ballot for their favorite. Remind them that their decision should be based on the creative way the songwriter sees and appreciates the goodness of God as the giver of life.

Date: _______________ Class/group: _______________

61
My Own Prayer

Ask each person to fold a piece of paper down the center. On the left side, write out the words of a favorite and well-known prayer such as the Our Father, Act of Faith, etc. On the right side, re-word that prayer with one's own personal understanding and words. Note the similarities and the differences. Note, too, that genuine prayer comes from our hearts and our own words help us to understand the words in the public prayers we use when we are all praying together. Encourage students to make up their own prayers.

Date: _______________ Class/group: _______________

62
Rain Days

A project which can remind students to think of the lonely and the shut-in is to prepare "rainy day cards" to be mailed "on a rainy day in April" to someone who is alone. The card should be of their own design and contain their own message. Remind them to include the offer to become a penpal if the receiver so wishes. Because people need to be needed, help the children think of ways to encourage responses in which the receivers have to share some wisdom, a bit of history, practical knowledge, etc.

Date: _______________ Class/group: _______________

63
Exultet

The Easter Proclamation in the Easter Saturday Vigil is filled with joy, gratitude, and history. Let older students use this *Exultet* as the basis for several minutes of quiet meditation. Then, ask them to express in poetry, prose, song, dance, or art, the phrase or phrases that struck them most deeply and moved them to a new understanding of the meaning of Jesus Risen. As these expressions may be deeply personal, ask permission before sharing them with others in the class.

Date: _______________ Class/group: _______________

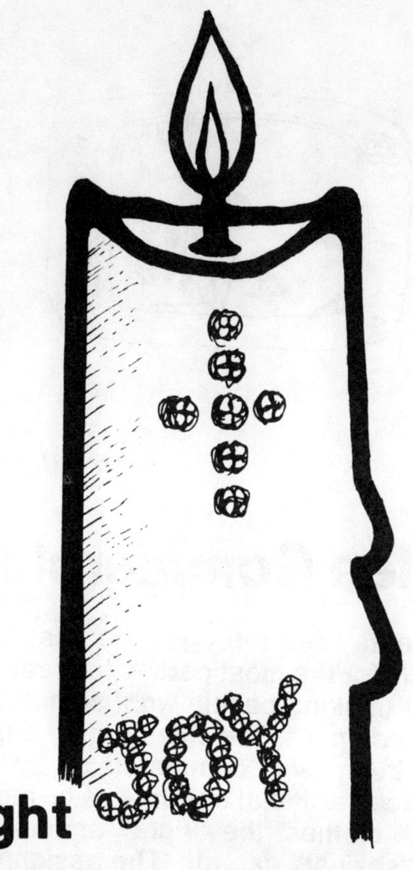

64
Life Light

During this season of the Pascal candle, encourage students to make their own candle as a reminder of the presence of the Risen Christ. After they obtain a stocky candle from a candle or gift shop, suggest such decorations as a cross made by inserting cloves into the candle, or decorator pins. Instead of a cross, they may wish to design words such as *Thanks, Joy, Life, Alive Forever,* etc. Ask each student to compose a one-line prayer to say when he or she uses the candle.

Date: _________________ Class/group: _________________

65
TeeHee Commercials

Help students "see through" the goal of TV commercials which, for the most part, is to create needs where none exist (making people want something they didn't want or need prior to the commercial). Encourage them to create their own "commercials" by poking fun at some of these artificial needs . . . e.g., the need to have the "right" clothes, the "right" shampoo, the "right" beer, the "sexiest" car, etc. The assignment demands the discipline of selecting a non-need and then dismissing it with a 30-second satire. The next time, transfer the creative energies toward selecting a genuine basic need of all people such as the need to be loved, respected, consoled, etc. and have them do a commercial to meet these authentic needs. They will discover that "products" may not do it but that human relationship and personal service will. Results can help them focus on genuine values.

Date: _________________ Class/group: _________________

66
Space Saver

If you are working with a group using a textbook, encourage the utmost concentration with a "space saver." Each person is to condense into one paragraph the key theme or content of the material being read. This forces a probing for the truth of the matter. It is also a good exercise to discipline the mind and also to help retain the core of what has been read.

Date: _________________ Class/group: _________________

67
Prayer of the Faithful

Catholic congregations are notoriously silent when they have an opportunity to pray aloud during Mass. To encourage this generation to take an active role in the liturgy, plan a *Prayer of the Faithful* time in class regularly with different students taking turns with the petitions. To get them started, you can begin with an introduction such as the priest uses and then remind the group to respond to each person's petition with "Hear our prayer, O Lord."

Date: _________________ Class/group: _________________

68
Scraps of Good News

Because each individual ultimately responds to God's word in his/her own way, try having the group make their own GOOD NEWS book. Ask each to bring an empty scrapbook to class. Spend some time with them explaining that God's word can change and transform us. Ask each to select a word, a phrase, or a short passage from the bible and to transfer it in a creative way to his/her own scrap book. Encourage them to illustrate the selected phrase or words with whatever has meaning for them. Continue to do this at various times during the year so that at the end of the school year, each student will have his/her own SCRAPS OF GOOD NEWS which have particular meaning for the individual. This is also a discovery process which helps the scrapbook's owner become more lovingly familiar with the bible.

Date: _______________ Class/group: _______________

69
The Lost Map

Since the majority of teens and adults have never read the Documents of Vatican II, select one or more of them, e.g., *The Constitution on the Church, Constitution on the Laity,* etc. and ask each member of the group to read the document looking for the key themes and important passages. Call it "The Lost Map" project and explain that each document provides a kind of map of life for us. Our task is to sketch out the main directions and roadsigns. Encourage the selection of favorite quotes from the readings to be saved for discussion at a following class.

Date: _________________ Class/group: _________________

70
Silver Jubilee

To help students realize that what we have now is largely a result of what others did before us, plan for a "silver jubilee." Assign each child to interview anyone in the parish with "silver" hair, asking such questions as "What was the church like when you were a child?" "What does Mass mean to you?" "What do you hope for the church in the future?" The "jubilee" part comes when all report back with the answers they received from the older members of the parish. A thank-you note written in class to each of those who were interviewed and delivered by hand on the following Sunday does wonders to make one generation feel appreciated by another and to create mutual interest in each group.

Date: _________________ Class/group: _________________

71
Adoption Option

Schedule a class or part of a class during which to plan an "Adoption Option" service activity. Ask each upper grade child to adopt a child in one of the early grades and become a big brother or big sister whose assignment is to help the young child learn correctly such basic prayers as *The Our Father, Hail Mary, Sign of the Cross,* and *Apostles' Creed.* The personal interest and support should encourage older students to appreciate what it means to be responsible for helping someone else.

Date: _______________ Class/group: _______________

72
The Invisible Kid

After teaching a class, place an empty chair in the front of the room and introduce the students to "the little boy who isn't there" sitting on the chair. Each student is to try to explain in a sentence or two what was learned in class to this "invisible kid" who needs to have everything explained very simply. Students who can accomplish this obviously have understood the lesson well and have made it their own. This technique helps teachers know whether their teaching was sufficiently clear.

Date: _______________ Class/group: _______________

73
My World

To help children understand who and where they are in history, have them make a collection of pictures or articles or headlines from newspapers and magazines. They are to select those which best illustrate, in mural form, the story of their lives up to the present. Then, have them make another mural of the world they hope to find themselves in about 10 years from now. Discuss these future world murals and what the students can actually do now to prepare for this world of hope in the future.

Date: _________________ Class/group: _________________

74
Praising Popes

Surprisingly, most Catholics know very little about the writing and teaching of our popes. Give each person or two or three grouped together, the names of the last five popes and ask them to return to class with one important paragraph, quotation, or teaching from these popes which expresses a gospel value our culture ignores. If you are specific and ask for statements on social justice, for example, your students may come to a new appreciation for the wise leadership and great statements the popes have made. This research will also create new questions about the historical periods in which each lived and how culture and theology are often intertwined.

Date: _________________ Class/group: _________________

75
Success Steps

Display or read insightful aphorisms from the wisdom books of the bible and from books of famous quotations. Then ask each to choose, find, or make up a "motto" for each step of the stairs in their homes. These should be printed on long wide strips of cardboard and pinned or tacked to the perpendicular part of each step. Needless to add, after the members of the family have seen them for several days, they may be taken down or changed, if the family likes the idea.

Date: _________________ Class/group: _________________

76
ABC-NBC-CBS Evening News

Appoint students to three groups in the class, and give them the assignment of being the ABC (NBC or CBS) EVENING NEWS team. They are to research, prepare, write, select, and program their news imitating the format and people of the company they represent. Their news has to include reports of key items learned in class, everyday events that reflect Gospel values, and interviews with people who are local heroes. The students may use tape recorders and present a completed program at the next class or may "go on live" having selected their own anchor man or woman and other reporters. Stress that the assignment is to encourage them to look for the good news that heralds the coming of the Kingdom of God.

Date: _________________ Class/group: _________________

77
Someone Else's Shoes

A technique that increases our awareness of others and of the uniqueness of each individual is this: Have the group take off their shoes and put them into a common pile. Then ask each person present to put on a pair that belongs to someone else. Now, try to be that other person whose shoes you are wearing. Think, hope, pray, and feel like that other person. A ten-minute meditation such as this will help students realize that we all have very much in common and that judging another is difficult if not impossible. Rash judgments and criticism disappear in relation to our understanding and loving acceptance of the other as he or she is. This activity works well when discussing the meaning of loving one another and the commandment not to bear false witness against one another.

Date: _________________ Class/group: _________________

78
Male/Female

Ask for adjectives which describe men or maleness and adjectives which describe women or femaleness. List these in two columns on the board. Now ask that each search the scriptures for the words, deeds, attitudes, and emotions of Jesus which are described by the *female* adjectives. This search should help get across the awareness that a totally human or complete person manifests the characteristics of both sexes. Once attention has been brought to this, it is amazing what the scriptures will then reveal to an alert reader. The ramifications for the future church become more and more obvious, too.

Date: _________________ Class/group: _________________

79
Bible Digest

A challenging assignment for teenagers is to have them study a favorite parable of Jesus. After it is selected, read, researched, and pondered over, ask them to condense into as few words as possible the important *meaning-for-me* of this parable. The discipline of honing the meaning down to the fewest words possible will stimulate them to really think through the essential meanings and get to the core of the message. Have them share their capsule quote with others to see if all agree that the selected words were adequately on target.

Date: ________________ Class/group: ________________

80
Prime Time

Recent polls indicate that most people pray informally and say "little prayers" many times a day. Hold a class discussion on prayer and encourage each student to write a "Prime Time" prayer or mantra of their very own. Suggest that they make this personal prayer their special "talking with God" reminder. Stress that these little moments of prayer are so important that they should become "prime time." Encourage many "prime times" during each day.

Date: ________________ Class/group: ________________

81
Design Day

Line drawings can sometimes be more expressive than words in attempting to convey how people image ideas.

Select a topic such as "Church" and tell the group that each is to design an image of how s/he prefers to image church for a highway poster contest. In the rules for this imaginary contest, tell them that their design should be clear enough so that people driving along the highway will get the message in a flash. If you are working with a very sophisticated group, suggest more abstract themes such as "salvation" "Grace" or one of the beatitudes.

Date: _______________ Class/group: _______________

82
Creation Days

Take time out to enjoy God's grandeur and beauty in spring and summer things. Ask the children to read Psalm18/19"The heavens declare the glory of God .." Then, take a class trip even if it is only 10 minutes around the block or down the street, to look carefully at the "glory of God and his handiwork." This could be done in silence. When they return to their seats, ask each child to compose his or her own psalm recounting what had been seen and appreciated during the walk. Encourage those who wish to, to share their psalms with the class so that the others can see how each individual sees life in a different way. End the class with Psalm 18/19 again. It will now have a much richer meaning.

Date: _______________ Class/group: _______________

83
Caught In the Act

Someone has said that if we were to stand trial for being Christian, very few of us would be convicted. The reason would be lack of evidence. Ask the children to react to that statement and then list four or five actions or activities which would definitely be a sign to others that they have been baptized and are committed to Christ and his way of life. This will prove to be more difficult than expected and should encourage a search through the New Testament. "How can we be caught in the act of being Christian" is the challenge each has to answer personally.

Date: _______________ Class/group: _______________

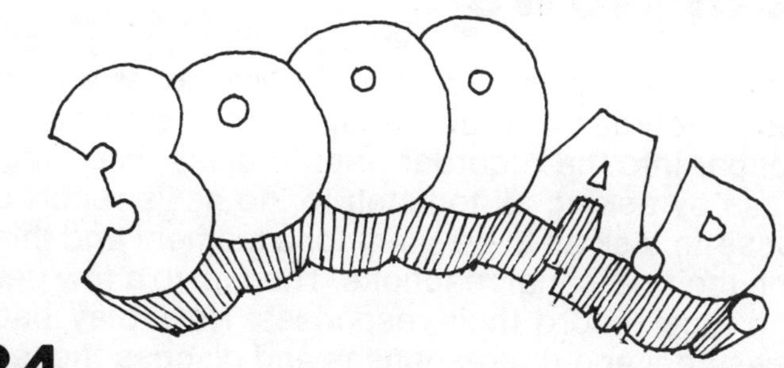

84
100 Years From Now

To help situate ourselves in history and become more aware that now is all we have and that every day we do the things that coalesce into who we will be forever, hand out blank sheets of paper. Ask each person to date the page with 3000 a.d. Now, ask each to write a one-page summary of who they are and how they could be recognized as Christian by what could be discovered about them by someone doing research in the year 3000 a.d. Presume that mocrofiche files and computer info will be available.

Date: _______________ Class/group: _______________

85
Local News

Tape a segment of the local news broadcast on your cassette recorder or read an important item from the newspaper into the recorder prior to class time. Begin the class by asking all to listen to the news report on the cassette. Ask all to be silent for a moment and think through their personal reactions. Then go to a few people and tape record their responses. Now, play back the news item and the responses and discuss these in class. The item selected should be a local problem that calls for a Christian response and the combined social action of all citizens. This project should encourage students to relate everyday events with Christ-values in the particular situation and bridge the still common "sacred-secular" gap.

Date: _______________ Class/group: _______________

86
Parent-Child Argument

Select a topic such as: Mass on Sunday, sharing a meal with a poor family, what percentage of the family money we should contribute to a special need, etc. and have the students divide into couples. One plays the role of the parent and the other plays the role of a child. Have them act out these topics as though they were being discussed at home. Let the rest of the class listen and then judge the argument. If there is time, choose another topic and the student who played the parent role is to play the child's role. This role-change gives the students a new experiential learning opportunity.

Date: _________________ Class/group: _________________

87
Seeing Jesus

Ask each member of the group to complete the sentence, "I see Jesus....." in a short phrase describing him. Collect the sentences of all and then read them aloud and have a reaction-discussion on how each person present can make the qualities listed part of his or her own personality. What it means to be Christlike will take on a new dimension after such an exercise. This activity will also lead the group to see how much more there is to know about Jesus.

Date: _________________ Class/group: _________________

88
Parish Council

In a class on responsible leadership, remind students that they may and can be representatives of the parish as members of their parish council in the future. Explore the different committees and the tasks belonging to each. Assign the class to attend a parish council meeting and then give a report and hold a discussion in the next class. Someone from the group should send a report to the Secretary of the Parish Council. Fireworks? Sometimes, but light and heat have lots of value.

Date: _________________ Class/group: _________________

89
The Real Agenda

If boredom is obvious in some groups, it could well be that the class subject matter needs to be evaluated. To insure a high interest response in your classes, ask each student to prepare a list of topics which s/he considers of prime importance in the lives of the group. Build your classes around the topics or themes which are most often mentioned in these lists and watch the results.

Date: _________________ Class/group: _________________

90
Filmstrip Party

The end of the year is a good time for a celebration which is also a review of the year's highlights. Appoint a committee to select the favorite filmstrips viewed during the year and prepare a "last class day" program during which some of these filmstrips are presented again and discussed. Encourage the students to invite family and friends as guests to share the celebration and to see and hear highlights of the year's classes. Cake and cookies also? Of course!

Date: _________________ Class/group: _________________

91
Summer Service

Help the members of your class become aware of the needy by assigning them to a *Summer Service Search.*

Obtain a list of organizations or groups in the parish who depend on volunteers. Each child or a team of children are to interview the officers of the organization and return to class with a report of what the group does and how the members of the class can participate during the summer vacation time. Organize an *ad hoc* summer club to assign volunteers to the group most in need of the service they can volunteer for at least a week during the summer.

Date: _________________ Class/group: _________________

92
Key Words

To help increase the consciousness and awareness levels of the group, ask each person to bring to the next class the most significant word that s/he can find in large bold type in a newspaper headline or a magazine head or ad. Paste this one word on a large sheet of paper and bring it to class. Have the group pass their papers around and have each write a phrase relating to the word on the paper. Then begin the search for significant meaning by having the originator of the word explain why s/he selected that word and how the phrases that the others in the group wrote relate to it or give the word a new and richer understanding. Note that shared insights enrich us all, a value that makes community salvific.

Date: _________________ Class/group: _________________

93
Reading Habits

Teens and adults can be helped by a group sharing of reading habits. Ask each person present to list the titles of books or magazines read during the past three months. Catagorize these into "complete reading with full attention," "casual reading" and "scanning." List these on the board or on butcher paper. The resulting discussion will highlight how our reading influences our way of life and our mores. The lack of reading of "anything Christian" will come as a surprise to many and opens up a prime opportunity for a creative teacher to introduce thoughtful people to the world of good periodicals and books.

Date: _________________ Class/group: _________________

94
The Good Old Days

Adults who resent change can be helped in the following way: Ask each member of the group to bring to the next meeting a very old catechism, spiritual reading, or "religious topic" book from their attic or dusty bookcase. Allow 20 minutes of silence during which time they are to "re-visit" these books and then have a discussion on the discoveries. For some, this will be a liberating experience and they will understand that change is part of life and that the "good old days" were only good in the same way that the "good now days" are good. The people present will want to exchange books after the discussion and they will want new books. Attentive teachers will have a display on hand or catalogs from publishers.

Date: _________________ Class/group: _________________

95
Good News in Different Words

Many people are unaware of the number of translations of the bible. Plan a meeting where at least a half dozen translations of the bible can be shared. Select a section such as the Sermon on the Mount or a parable or the priestly prayer of Jesus at the Last Supper, etc. Have different members of the group read from the various translations while the rest of the class sit with eyes closed in silence. After a period of reflection, have an exchange on how different phrases meant so much more (or less) to the listeners than the translation which was most familiar to them. This exercise leads into a new appreciation for biblical research and a desire for more familiarity with scripture.

Date: _________________ Class/group: _________________

96
My Obituary

In order to focus on the meaning of life, on goals, on hopes for the future, ask each person to write his or her own obituary notice for the local paper and what s/he might like to have on the tombstone. This is a difficult assignment but results in a realistic look at life and the importance of aiming at goals rather than drifting into the future.

Date: _________________ Class/group: _________________

97
Flee Market

A project that can be challenging for all grade levels as well as adults is a *flea* market designed to be a *flee* market. In order to help people *flee* from becoming lost in a consumer society and to encourage them to share the things they really do not need, ask each person to bring some contribution to a flea market for a class project. The contribution has to be important to the giver. Offerings may be auctioned off and the proceeds donated to a specific need or charitable organization. The purpose of the project is not so much to make money as it is to help individuals experience that "letting go" is a freeing thing.

Date: _________________ Class/group: _________________

98
Next Year

During a May or a June class, assign for homework a letter to be written to a parent or relative. It should contain a report on what was studied, appreciated, celebrated during the current school year. Then, ask each to write a P.S. "Next year, I want to know more about ________. I would also like to ________. The filled-in blanks will give the teacher a guide to where to begin in the fall. It also helps children see that religious formation is a lifelong process and doesn't end with the school year.

Date: ________________ Class/group: ________________

99
Updating Parables

After a study of the parables, ask each to select a favorite and then rewrite it in contemporary terms. These terms should reflect the experiences, language, and influences of the culture or ethnic group of the writer. Have a "parable hour" in which each reads his or her updated parable. Permit time to react to each of these and reflect on how the basic truth applies to all generations at all times in history.

Date: ________________ Class/group: ________________

100
Contentment

Each catechist is entitled to a "contentment hour": take time out to reflect on the good you are doing and be grateful for the opportunity to do so. Recall how important it is to have teachers who witness to truth in your own life and realize that you are this witness to the group that you teach and share your faith with in word and action. Your contentment hour is your time of gratitude to God for calling you to share your faith in Him with others.

MINI MEDITATION MUSINGS

Am I a good teacher? I look at Jesus and note some of his qualities. He was:

Available

"And they came to a house and the multitude came together again, so that they could not so much as eat bread." (Mark 3:20) Jesus was always available to those who came to him and they came continuously. Am I available to my students on an individual basis?

Compassionate

"And seeing the multitudes, he had compassion on them, because they were distressed and lying like sheep that have no shepherd." (Matt. 9:36) Am I sympathetic and compassionate when my students come to me for a focus, for a guide to good decisions?

Humble

"And I know His commandment is eternal life. So, whatever I speak, I speak as the Father has told me." (John 12:50) Am I concerned to pass on his good news, not putting myself and my private concerns in between the student and the message I have the privilege of sharing? And when I don't know answers to questions, do I humbly promise to find the answer, if possible, for the next time I see them?

Joyful

"These things I have spoken to you, that My joy may be in you, and your joy may be full." (John 15:11) Am I a joy-filled teacher so that my students catch my attitude as well as my message?

Patient

"Have I been so long a time with you and you have not known me? Philip, he that sees me sees the Father also. How can you say, show us the Father?" (John 14:9) After three years of teaching his apostles, Jesus was still getting "dumb" questions. Do I imitate Christ's patience when students ask questions which indicate they have not paid the least bit of attention to what I was teaching?

Prudent

"Wherefore Jesus walked no more openly among the Jews, but He went into a country near the desert." (John 11:54) Prudence sometimes may call for a curtailment of activities, even when they seem to be necessary and right. To avoid a scene, it is better to be silent for the time being. Prudence can prevent problems from arising. How tactful, balanced, and prudent am I?

Loving

"Suffer children to come to me, and forbid them not; for of such is the kingdom of God." (Luke 18:16) The magnetic quality which draws people to good teachers is their *love* far more than their skill in communicating or educating. Do my students know that I love them?

Other Recommended Teacher Resources

From

Twenty-Third Publications

A Book for All Seasons. By Carl Pfeifer and Janaan
Manternach. 1977. $3.50

Monthly helps and hints for catechists in five types of
aids: planning calendars, memo book, celebrations,
journal, personal renewal and inspiration. All in this
helpful book.

Celebrations for Children. By Fred Thompson. 1978. $5.95

Teacher aid to create exciting and memorable Eucharistic celebrations. Illustrated to clearly show all preparation details. Practical resource information included.

Jesus Plays for Primary Grades. By Dorinda Clark. 1978. $2.95

Bible-inspired teaching plays for the classroom bring Jesus to life for primary grades. Simple prop suggestions and imaginative illustrations help you create atmosphere for happy plays.

Lifelines for Religion Teachers. By Anne Cooke, S.S.J.

Twenty classroom activities for teaching and reinforcing bible study with a minimum of materials, for grades 1-9. Model lesson plans follow successful 'Workshop Way to Learning.'

Parish Youth Ministry. By Bill and Patty Coleman. 1977. $7.95

A Beginner's Manual for those getting involved in youth ministry work on the parish or school level. Models of programs for teens, resource listings and practical background readings.

The Religion Teacher-Learner. By Margaret Timmerman, MHSH. 1975. $2.95

Now in its fourth printing, this is a proven self-help guide suitable for teachers to use on their own or in groups to evaluate and improve their teaching skills and techniques.

Teaching the Church Today. By Carl Pfeifer. 1978. $3.50

Historical and cultural view of the Church with specific graded approaches to incorporate this rich heritage and identity into classroom lessons and activities. All levels.

Teaching the Ten Commandments Today. By Carl Middleton and Robert Craig. 1977. $4.95

Just the extra help needed to understand the Ten Commandments and then to incorporate them properly into classroom catechetics. All levels.

World Religions. By Dorothy Dixon. 1977. $1.95

Chapter by chapter treatment of each major world religion plus discussion questions and bibliography for each. Intermediate through adult levels.

World Religions for the Classroom. By Dorothy A. Dixon, Ph.D. 1975. $19.95

Huge 400-page volume (with 200 pages you are allowed to photocopy for class use) illuminates the world of wonder and imagination for intermediate and junior-high students as they see how others believe and live.

Invaluable Monthly Help for all Religion Teachers

Religion Teacher's Journal magazine for practical classroom ideas, better lesson preparation, spiritual nurture, and general all-around enrichment for beginning and experienced teachers alike. Available in single subscriptions for 1 year (8 issues) or at discounts for parish bulk subscriptions.

Filmstrips Especially for Children

The Parables. By Ed and Maureen Curley $19.95 per strip

The best known parables of Jesus are recast in contemporary form while remaining true to biblical specifics. Each filmstrip has three stories, two in color and photography and one in cartoon form. Primary 1: Unjust Steward, Vineyard Workers, Rich Man & Lazarus; Primary 2: Lamp & Bushel, Good Shepherd, Good Samaritan; Primary 3: Great Banquet, Dragnet, The Two Sons; Intermediate 1: The Talents, Wheat & Cockle, The Sower; Intermediate 2: Pharisee & Publican, Prodigal Son, The Great Supper.

The Our Father. By Ed Curley $19.95

For lower grades the goal is learning the Our Father. For upper grades the biblical heritage reflected through the themes of praise, hope, forgiveness, and redemption are portrayed through vignettes of Daniel, Noah, Joseph and Lot. All in full color cartoon style with an in-depth teacher guide.

Holydays and Holidays. By James Haas. Ill. by Ed Curley $39.95

Four cartoon filmstrip stories capture the meanings of Easter, Christmas, Thanksgiving and Halloween for primary and intermediate grades. A teacher guide elicits Christian values.

Reconciliation and Penance. By Janaan Manternach & Carl Pfeifer $39.95

This two-filmstrip program presents the concepts of sin and reconciliation for children through middle grades. Use for sacrament preparation or review. A study guide, script and an actual reconciliation service is included.

NEED HELP IN A HURRY?
PHONE 1-203-536-2611
AND ORDER YOUR
CATECHETICAL SUPPLIES
QUICKLY!
DRES ARE HUMAN, TOO
M.R.